THE OFFICIAL
CHELS[EA] [F]C
ANNUAL 2010

Written By Rick Glanvill

Designed By Alice Lake-Hammond

A Grange Publication

© 2009. Published by Grange Communications Ltd., Edinburgh, under licence from Chelsea FC Merchandising Limited, www.chelseafc.com.

Photographs © Getty Images & Press Association Images

ISBN 978-1-906211-76-9

£6.99

CONTENTS 2010

CIAO CARLO!

Remember, 'ciao' means hello as well as goodbye. And the arrival of Signor Ancelotti as manager found us in Italian mood when we were putting together the latest Official Chelsea FC Annual.

With every article there was a sprinkle of Parmesan cheese, no quiz question was created without a tub of Neapolitan ice cream, and we all said 'Bravo!' when we finished the final pages.

Hopefully, you will enjoy reading this as much as we enjoyed putting it together.

2010 is a World Cup year, and Stamford has been busy thinking about what a brilliant event that will be and we take a look back at some Chelsea men who starred at previous tournaments.

We also celebrate the anniversary of one of Chelsea's most famous victories: the 1970 FA Cup.

There is a whole lot more besides, all about your favourite football club.

Have fun!

SEASON REVIEW

17 August 2008
A GREAT START

New boss Luiz Felipe Scolari was an instant hit when his side played wicked football and beat Pompey 4-0 on the first day of the season. It was the same result a few weeks later at Fratton Park – in the Carling Cup.

16 September 2008
LOOKING GOOD IN EUROPE

The mighty Blues were off to a flier in the Champions League too. Frank Lampard's goal (pictured) helped humble Bordeaux 4-0 at the Bridge. Looking back it was an amazing result – Laurent Blanc's team went on to win the French league title.

5 October 2008
MOST MISSED

Joe Cole was injured against Southend United in January – and didn't we miss the kind of trickery he always delivers. Here he is cracking in the opener during our 2-0 league win over Aston Villa.

18 Oct 2008
HITTING THE NET

We scored tons of goals in the first part of the season, and set a record for our best ever win away to Middlesbrough. It finished 5-0, with Lamps grabbing a rare diving header.

26 October 2008
END OF THE RECORD

It was a shock when we lost our proud unbeaten record at Stamford Bridge to Liverpool. Still, we had gone a massive 86 matches without defeat – much more than any other club has ever managed, and something to be proud of.

8 December 2008
ROCK OF THE SEASON

When results started to go wrong for the Blues one player held everything together on the pitch, our skipper JT. He inspired his team-mates when times were tough and helped lead the revival under Guus in the new year. Top man.

14 December 2008
GOLDEN BOOT

We saw the 'butterfly' celebration a lot this season! Nico, pictured after scoring against West Ham, also grabbed two hat-tricks in matches and eventually topped the Premier League scorers list with 19.

SEASON REVIEW

17 January 2009

LATE, LATE SHOW

How much did we all celebrate when Frank whacked in the winner at home to Stoke to complete a 2-1 comeback? It came in the final stoppage-time minute of his 400th Chelsea appearance and, as you can see, the whole stadium went bonkers.

17 January 2009

IMPACT SUBS...

Let's not forget that two 19-year-olds came off the bench to change the game against Stoke. Franco Di Santo set up the equaliser, and Miroslav Stoch's right-wing trickery led eventually to Lamps' winner.

14 February 2009

CUP DEBUTANT

Another Academy graduate, Michael Mancienne, made a stylish start to his Chelsea career in the FA Cup replay at Watford. JT was suspended, so the England Under-21 replaced Branislav Ivanovic at right-back. A few days later he looked the business against Juve.

7 March 2009
COMEBACK KING

How different would the end of the season have been without Michael Essien's early return from his knee injury? And how much better would the rest of the season been if he had been available?

8 April 2009
HEADERS OF THE SEASON
Branislav Ivanovic stunned Liverpool in the Champions League with not one, but two powerful headed goals! The 6'2" Serbia defender's first goals for us put the Blues 2-1 up in the tie and left Chelsea fans the only ones singing at Anfield.

14 April 2009
UNSUNG HERO

With Riccy Carvalho injured for long periods, Alex stepped in brilliantly as John Terry's partner. With his powerful defending and crucial goals (including this one against Liverpool in the Champions League semi) fans took the Brazilian to their hearts.

28 April 2009
STILL WORLD CLASS

Cech has proved time and again that he is the best in the world. In Barça's Camp Nou he kept a clean sheet with stunning saves against Henry, Alves, Eto'o and Hleb.

SEASON REVIEW

2 May 2009
EARLY BIRD

The Blues' fastest strike of the season came against Fulham, when Guus played Nico and the Drog in attack together. Nico scored after just 51 seconds and celebrated with his strike partner.

6 May 2009
GOAL OF THE SEASON

It has almost been forgotten because of the result, but Michael Essien's amazing volley at home to Barcelona was our goal of the season. It deserved to win any match.

6 May 2009
HEARTBREAK

It still hurts, doesn't it? We all felt the same despair as JT and Juliano Belletti when Iniesta scored that stoppage time equalizer. It was enough to take Barça through to the Champions League final on the 'away goals' rule.

10 May 2009
MATCH OF THE SEASON

It's always a laugh when we beat Arsenal, even better on their home patch, and extra special when it's a 4-1 win! Ash takes a lot of stick from their fans, so he had even more reason to celebrate with Lamps at the final whistle.

17 May 2009
MOST IMPROVED PLAYER

Florent Malouda had a fantastic end to the season under Guus. At times down the left flank, especially against Arsenal, Barcelona, Blackburn and Everton, he was unstoppable. Well done FloMo!

17 May 2009
CHANT OF THE SEASON

Everyone at Chelsea will miss Guus Hiddink, but especially the fans. At the final home game against Blackburn the Dutchman bowed to all four stands after supporters sang: 'We want you to stay!'

30 May 2009
SILVERWARE

We love the FA Cup at Chelsea, and no club has been to the new Wembley Stadium more. The final this season was a great day out, with the perfect result to the game – 2-1 to the Blues – and to the end of the season.

MEET THE MANAGER
CIAO CARLO!

On 1 July 2009 Carlo Ancelotti became Chelsea's new manager. He is the Blues' third manager from Italy, after Gianluca Vialli and Claudio Ranieri, and has spent his entire football career in his home country. So here's our guide to the new boss of the Blues.

- **10 June 1959** Carlo was born in Reggiolo, in the middle of northern Italy.
- **1976** His career as a professional footballer started at Parma, as a hard-working midfielder, and he moved to Roma three years later.
- **1980** He won his first silverware with Roma, the Coppa Italia (their version of the FA Cup). Carlo and Roma won the cup again in 1981, 1984 and 1986.
- **1983** Carlo and Roma won Serie A, the Italian premier league.
- **1987/88** Carlo joined the famous AC Milan, who won Serie A in his debut season.
- **1989** Carlo was in the Milan team that won the European Cup by slaughtering Steaua Bucharest 4-0 in the final. It is reckoned to be one of the greatest teams Europe has ever produced. Milan won the cup again the following season.

> "There will be the same pressure at Chelsea because Chelsea and Milan are great teams in Europe and they want to win all the competitions."

Here's AC Milan celebrating victory in the 1989 European Cup. Carlo Ancelotti is the one crouching slightly with his hand on the trophy. The legendary team also included future Chelsea player and manager Ruud Gullit (with dreadlocks), Frank Rijkaard, Marco van Basten and Paolo Maldini.

"Chelsea have a great record [in the Champions League]. Five semi-finals in six years is a beautiful score, but now we have to win it. The Champions League for me is the best competition in the world and everyone wants to win it."

1990 Milan retain European title with a 1-0 win over Benfica. Ancelotti is part of the Italy squad for the 1990 World Cup on home soil, where they lose in the semi-finals to Argentina.

1991 Carlo won the last of his 26 Italy caps, and a year later he retired from playing when Milan won Serie A again.

1995/96 His first management post was at Serie B club Reggiana, who he led immediately to promotion to Serie A.

1996/97 Carlo moved to Parma, immediately selling Gianfranco Zola to Chelsea, but then coaching his side to second place in Serie A.

1998/99 Carlo joined Juventus as manager, building his team around Zinedine Zidane, and just missed out on Serie A titles, before joining Milan in 2001.

2003 AC Milan win the Champions League by beating Juventus in the final at Old Trafford. The following season Milan won the league title.

2005 Carlo was shocked when his Milan team squandered a 3-0 half-time lead in the Champions League final against Liverpool. The Reds levelled the score at 3-3 and won on penalties.

2007 It was Liverpool in the Champions League final again, but this time Milan win easily, 2-1.

31 May 2009 Having steered Milan to a Champions League place finish in Serie A, Carlo leaves Italy and signs a three-year contract with Chelsea the following day.

As coach of AC Milan, Carlo Ancelotti celebrated winning the Champions League at the Olympic Stadium in Athens. They beat Liverpool 2-1.

The coach of Russia's national team, Guus Hiddink, arrived at Stamford Bridge in February 2009 to help out his friend, the Chelsea owner Roman Abramovich, by managing our club till the end of the season. First he watched in the stands as Chelsea – coached by his assistant Ray Wilkins – demolished Watford 3-1 in the FA Cup, then he led the Blues superbly all the way to the FA Cup final, to the semi-final of the Champions League, and to automatic European qualification in 2009/10. His time in charge began with the best EVER start in the league by a Chelsea boss. Having completed his mission, he headed back to Moscow to prepare for the World Cup, as planned. Everyone loved the brilliant Dutchman – and he loved us right back! Good luck in the future, Guus – you're welcome at the Bridge anytime.

Continental Roast!

50 Years of European Competition

On 30 September 1958, Chelsea played their first ever competitive match against European opposition. Chelsea's continental debut was against BK Frem in Copenhagen, Denmark.

The Blues won 3-1, and triumphed in the home leg 4-1 – Jimmy Greaves scoring twice. Manager Ted Drake steered them to the quarter-finals where they met Ville De Belgrade, an all-star team from the Yugoslavian capital. Belgrade proved too strong and our first European competition was over. The media were not much bothered about these games back then. Fifty years on, Uefa tournaments are covered by more TV companies and newspapers around the world than any other.

Here is our continental selection from five decades of European competition.

Chelsea's first European trophy arrived in May 1971, when we beat the mighty Real Madrid 2-1 in a Uefa Cup-Winners' Cup replay in Athens. Huge crowds welcomed the winners home.

May 1971

Gianfranco Zola scored the only goal against Stuttgart in the 1998 final that brought the Uefa Cup-Winners' Cup back to Stamford Bridge.

May 1998

The Super Cup is played in Monaco between the two teams that win the previous season's Uefa competitions. In August 1998 Chelsea beat Real Madrid – again – with a goal from Gustavo Poyet (pictured).

August 1998

1955/56

As league champions, Chelsea should have made history by entering the first ever European Cup (now the Champions League) in 1955/56. This is the man who blocked us: Football League secretary, Alan Hardaker. He argued that European Cup matches would cause fixture congestion. What an old fogey!

One of the most amazing nights ever at Stamford Bridge came in the 2004/05 Champions League. Skipper John Terry headed a late goal against Barcelona to send Chelsea through with a 4-2 win.

March 2005

May 1958

Did you know that a Chelsea player scored against Barcelona in the final of a European competition, but he wasn't playing for Chelsea? The goal was by the great Jimmy Greaves (pictured) and the occasion was the final of the first Inter-Cities Fairs Cup (later called the Uefa Cup), in which all-star teams from cities across Europe took part. Amazingly, the competition extended over three seasons, not one, from 1955 to 1958. The 'London XI', managed by Chelsea chairman Joe Mears, included Greaves, fellow Blue Peter Sillett, and players from Arsenal, Fulham and Spurs. Jimmy scored in the first leg, which ended 2-2, but Barcelona won in Spain 6-0!

BLUE SAID THAT?

There was plenty to talk about again last season, and we've picked out some of the things people said about Chelsea. But can you work out who said what?

1

"I have already beaten Barcelona twice – in my head."

2

"We will try everything to get (defending at set-pieces) right: zonal, man-to-man, sticking a coach in front of it, we will try the lot until we get the right solution."

3

"For me Didier Drogba is an all-round player and a complete striker. In the form he is in there is no better striker out there, the way he shrugs people off and runs through. He is the best out there for me."

4

"This is the best one (FA Cup medal) and means the most because I am with my real friends and I am at a great club here."

5

"I ran to Mikel because he told me I would score (against Barcelona) when we were having lunch. I said if I did I would run over to him and hug him."

Answers P.60

ALEX

Born: Niterói, Brazil, 17.6.82
Height: 1.89m (6ft 2in)
Weight: 92kgs (14st 7lb)
Previous clubs: Atlético Juventus, Santos, PSV Eindhoven
Signed: August 2007
Chelsea debut: Liverpool (a) 19.8.07, substitute for Florent Malouda. Drew 1-1.

NICOLAS ANELKA

Born: Versailles, France, 14.3.79
Height: 1.85m (6ft 1in)
Weight: 83.5kgs (13st 2lb)
Previous clubs: Paris Saint Germain, Arsenal, Real Madrid, Paris Saint Germain, Liverpool (loan), Manchester City, Fenerbahce, Bolton Wanderers
Signed: January 2008
Chelsea debut: Tottenham (h) 12.1.08, substitute for Claudio Pizarro. Won 2-0.

MICHAEL BALLACK

Born: Görlitz, Germany, 26.9.76
Height: 1.88m (6ft 2in)
Weight: 89kgs (14st 1lb)
Previous clubs: Chemnitz, Kaiserslautern, Bayer Leverkusen, Bayern Munich
Signed: May 2006
Chelsea debut: Liverpool (Millennium Stadium) FA Community Shield 13.8.06. Lost 1-2.

JULIANO BELLETTI

Born: Cascavel, Brazil, 20.6.76
Height: 1.79m (5ft 10in)
Weight: 76.5kgs (12st 1lb)
Previous clubs: Cruzeiro, Sao Paulo, Atlético Mineiro (loan), Villarreal, Barcelona
Signed: August 2007
Chelsea debut: Portsmouth (h) 25.8.07, substitute for John Mikel Obi. Won 1-0.

JOSÉ BOSINGWA

Born: Mbandaka, Democratic Republic of Congo, 24.8.82
Height: 1.83m (6ft)
Weight: 72kgs (11st 5lb)
Previous clubs: Boavista, SC Freamunde (loan), Porto
Signed: May 2008
Chelsea debut: Portsmouth (h) 17.8.08. Won 4-0.

RICARDO CARVALHO

Born: Amarante, Portugal, 18.5.78
Height: 1.81m (5ft 11in)
Weight: 78kgs (12st 4lb)
Previous clubs: Amarante, Leça, Porto, Vitória Setúbal (loan), Alverca (loan)
Signed: July 2004
Chelsea debut: Man Utd (h) 15.8.04, substitute for Gérémi. Won 1-0.

DID YOU KNOW... Alex scored Chelsea's 1,000th Premier League goal in 2008/09.

PETR CECH

Born: Plzen, Czech Republic, 20.5.82
Height: 1.96m (6ft 5in)
Weight: 89.5kgs (14st 1lb)
Previous clubs: Viktoria Plzen, Chmel Blsany, Sparta Prague, Rennes
Signed: July 2004
Chelsea debut: Man Utd (h) 15.8.04. Won 1-0.

ASHLEY COLE

Born: Stepney, 20.12.80
Height: 1.76m (5ft 9in)
Weight: 64kgs (10st 1lb)
Previous clubs: Arsenal, Crystal Palace (loan)
Signed: August 2006
Chelsea debut: Charlton (h) 9.9.06, substitute for Wayne Bridge. Won 2-1.

PLAYER PROFILES

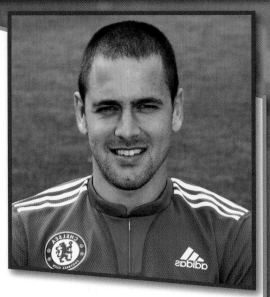

JOE COLE

Born: Islington, 8.11.81
Height: 1.76m (5ft 9in)
Weight: 73kgs (11st 7lb)
Previous club: West Ham
Signed: August 2003
Chelsea debut: MŠK Žilina (a) Champions League 3rd Qualifying Rd 13.8.03, substitute for Damien Duff. Won 2-0.

DECO

Born: São Bernardo do Campo, Brazil, 27.8.77
Height: 1.74m (5ft 8in)
Weight: 76kgs (11st 13lb)
Previous clubs: Nacional, Corinthians, Corinthians Alagoano, Benfica, Alverca (loan), Salgueiros, Porto, Barcelona.
Signed: July 2008
Chelsea debut: Portsmouth (h) 17.8.08. Won 4-0, scored the final goal.

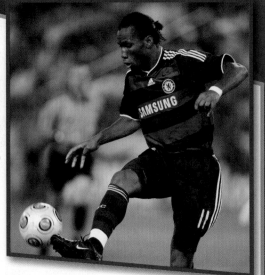

DIDIER DROGBA

Born: Abidjan, Ivory Coast, 11.3.78
Height: 1.89m (6ft 2in)
Weight: 91kgs (14st 5lb)
Previous clubs: Leval, Le Mans, Guingamp, Marseille
Signed: July 2004
Chelsea debut: Man Utd (h) 15.8.04. Won 1-0.

MICHAEL ESSIEN

Born: Accra, Ghana, 3.12.82
Height: 1.77m (5ft 10in)
Weight: 85.5kgs (13st 6lb)
Previous clubs: Liberty Professionals (Ghana), Bastia, Lyon
Signed: August 2005
Chelsea debut: Arsenal (h) 21.8.05, substitute for Eidur Gudjohnsen. Won 1-0.

PAULO FERREIRA

Born: Cascais, Portugal, 18.1.79
Height: 1.83m (6ft)
Weight: 76kgs (11st 13lb)
Previous clubs: Alcabideche, Cascais, Estoril, Vitória Setúbal, Porto
Signed: July 2004
Chelsea debut: Man Utd (h) 15.8.04. Won 1-0.

HILÁRIO

Born: São Pedro da Cova, Portugal, 21.10.75
Height: 1.89m (6ft 2in)
Weight: 88kgs (13st 12lb)
Previous clubs: Porto, Académica de Coimbra (loan), Nacional
Signed: May 2006
Chelsea debut: Barcelona (h) Champions League 18.10.06. Won 1-0.

DID YOU KNOW... Michael Essien has won Goal of the Season twice at Chelsea.

SAM HUTCHINSON

Born: Slough, 3.08.89
Height: 1.83m (6ft)
Weight: 77.5kgs (12st 3lb)
Previous clubs: none
Chelsea debut: Everton (h) 13 May 2007, substitute for Wayne Bridge.

BRANISLAV IVANOVIC

Born: Sremska Mitrovica, Serbia, 22.2.84
Height: 1.85m (6ft 1in)
Weight: 89kgs (14st 1lb)
Previous clubs: SREM Sremska Mitrovica, OFK Beograd, Lokomotiv Moscow
Signed: January 2008
Chelsea debut: Portsmouth (a) League Cup 24.9.08. Won 4-0.

PLAYER PROFILES

SALOMON KALOU

Born: Oumé, Ivory Coast, 5.8.85
Height: 1.86m (6ft 1in)
Weight: 78.5kgs (12st 5lb)
Previous clubs: Feyenoord, Excelsior (loan)
Signed: May 2006
Chelsea debut: Liverpool (Millennium Stadium) FA Community Shield 13.8.06, substitute for Michael Ballack. Lost 1-2.

FRANK LAMPARD

Born: Romford, 20.6.78
Height: 1.84m (6ft)
Weight: 88kgs (13st 12lb)
Previous clubs: West Ham, Swansea (loan)
Signed: June 2001
Chelsea debut: Newcastle (h) 19.08.01. Drew 1-1.

FLORENT MALOUDA

Born: Cayenne, F. Guiana, 13.6.80
Height: 1.77m (5ft 10in)
Weight: 80kgs (12st 8lb)
Previous clubs: Châteauroux, Guingamp, Lyon
Signed: July 2007
Chelsea debut: Man Utd (Wembley) FA Community Shield 5.8.07. Lost 0-3 on penalties after a 1-1 draw in normal time. Scored the equalising goal.

JOHN MIKEL OBI

Born: Jos, Nigeria, 22.4.87
Height: 1.88m (6ft 2in)
Weight: 86kgs (13st 8lb)
Previous clubs: Plateau United, Ajax Cape Town, Lyn Oslo
Signed: June 2006
Chelsea debut: Liverpool (Millennium Stadium) FA Community Shield 13.8.06, substitute for Paulo Ferreira.

DANIEL STURRIDGE

Born: Birmingham, 1.09.89
Height: 1.89m (6ft 2in)
Weight: 76kgs (12st)
Previous clubs: Manchester City.

JOHN TERRY

Born: Barking, 7.12.80
Height: 1.87m (6ft 2in)
Weight: 90.5kgs (14st 3lb)
Source: Chelsea Academy
Turned pro: March 1998
Chelsea debut: Aston Villa (h) League Cup
28.10.98, substitute for Dan Petrescu. Won
4-1.

DID YOU KNOW... Frank Lampard is the highest-scoring midfielder in Chelsea's history.

ROSS TURNBULL

Born: Bishop Auckland, 4.01.85
Height: 1.93m (6ft 4in)
Weight: 85kgs (13st 4lb)
Previous clubs: Middlesbrough, Darlington
(loan), Barnsley (loan), Bradford City (loan),
Crewe (loan), Cardiff (loan).

YURI ZHIRKOV

Born: Tambov, Russia, 20.08.83
Height: 1.85m (6ft 1in)
Weight: 75kgs (11st 11lb)
Previous clubs: Spartak Tambov, CSKA
Moscow

YOUNG LIONS!

Who will be next to break through at Chelsea? Here, we pick some of the young Blues who have shone in 2008/09.

Josh McEACHRAN

Jack CORK

Born 1 March 1993 in Oxford

Sixteen-year-old Josh McEachran is a schoolboy playing above his age group for England under-17s and already catching people's eyes. Small, nippy and able to take on and beat opponents at will, the left-sided attacking midfielder likes to set up chances and take a few himself.

"Josh, technically, is way above his year," says youth team manager Dermot Drummy. "We don't play him the full game most of the time and our conditioning coaches are working on programmes to build his body up to stand the rigours of the football - but he's an exciting talent."

Assistant First Team Coach Paul Clement agrees: "Worth another mention is Josh McEachran, a schoolboy who trains three days a week with us, plays regularly in the youth team and recently captained England under-16s, so he is making nice progress."

Also watch out for: defender Jeffrey Bruma, central midfielder Conor Clifford.

Born 25 June 1989 in Carshalton, Surrey

Son of Wimbledon legend Alan, versatile midfielder Jack Cork has earned rave reviews in 44 games on loan at Southampton and Watford, where he helped former Academy boss Brendan Rodgers steer clear of relegation. He was the Hornets' star player, but was unable to play against the Blues in the FA Cup – luckily for us!

"It was a hard decision [to join Watford]," admitted the 19-year-old, "because the Southampton fans were all right with me, but Brendan being at Watford made it a good choice."

Jack sees a lot of value in playing plenty of games and dealing with different teams and tactical approaches: "My year at Scunthorpe was good last year and having to settle in somewhere new, not just football but for life in general, it is good for you."

Jack went out on loan to Coventry for the first half of Season 2009/10.

Others to watch: skilful attacking midfielder Gael Kakuta, versatile left-sider Ryan Bertrand.

Patrick van AANHOLT

Born 29 August 1990
in 's-Hertogenbosch, Holland

Flying Dutchman Patrick, 18, has just signed a new three-year contract with Chelsea. He started his career at PSV Eindhoven in his native country when Guus Hiddink was in charge of the senior squad. He started life at Cobham playing as an Ashley Cole-style attacking left-back, but has since also adapted to the left midfield position, where his fierce pace and direct passing are more dangerous. A wicked shot against Aston Villa reserves revealed a new skill at free kicks too.

Sporting Director Frank Arnesen says of Patrick: "He had a good first year with us but really kicked on last season, especially the last six months. He is very quick, turns fast, has a good leap and is good in one-on-ones with attackers.
"Although he is not yet the same physically, you can compare him to Ashley Cole: Patrick has all the attributes for the modern full-back. Most important, he is willing to learn all the time. He needs to keep that mentality to reach the best team in the world - Chelsea."

Patrick went out on loan to Coventry for the first half of the 2009/10 season.

Others to watch: midfielder Jacob Mellis, centre-forward Fabio Borini.

2008/09 Chelsea Academy international appearances

Ryan Bertrand
(England U19s 3, U20s 1) 4
Fabio Borini
(Italy U19s) 2
Jeffrey Bruma
(Holland U19s) 3+1
Conor Clifford
(Rep of Ireland U19s) 5+2
Jack Cork
(England U19s) 3
Aliu Djalo
(Portugal U17s) 8+4
Nic Heimann
(Germany U18s) 1
Gael Kakuta
(France U18s) 4+1
Billy Knott
(England U17s) 4+2
Milan Lalkovic
(Slovakia U17s) 3
Josh McEachran
(England U17s) 1
Jacob Mellis
(England U19s) 1
Marco Mitrovic
(Sweden U17s) 5
Morten Nielsen
(Denmark U19s) 8+1
Fabio Paim
(Portugal U20s) 1
Jacopo Sala
(Italy U19s) 2
Scott Sinclair
(England U19s 1+2, U20s 1) 2+2
Miroslav Stoch
(Slovakia U20s) 1
Rhys Taylor
(Wales U19s) 2
Gokhan Tore
(Turkey U17s) 3
Patrick van Aanholt
(Holland U19s) 5
Michael Woods
(England U19s) 3+2

YOU CAN'T BEAT A BIRTHDAY BASH AT THE BRIDGE

Too young for paintball, bored of ten-pin bowling? How about a party at the Bridge next time it's your big day?

Every weekend when there is no match at Stamford Bridge, the place is still alive with the sound of cheering – at children's parties. The club has organised birthday packages for years, and now they're as popular as ever. You get to hear all the stories about Chelsea's famous stadium on a tour, have a game of football too, and get a Chelsea gift at the end.

Wesley Barton, the Chelsea FC Stadium Tours and Museum Supervisor, is part of the team that makes sure everything runs smoothly and everyone enjoys themselves on the day.

"It really is a unique opportunity to go on the tour of the stadium with your mates, and play football on our inflatable pitch," says Wes, "which is always great fun."

Guess what is usually the highlight of the day.

"It's definitely the football generally," laughs Wes. "It goes down the best with the party-goers and – you never know – I may even show you a few silky skills if you're lucky!"

The parties are organised when there is no football taking place because on matchdays every room in the stadium is packed with supporters, guests and players – you get to see where they hang out on the tour!

"Quite a few famous parents have had their children's parties with us at the Bridge," reveals Wes. "We've even organised them for the children of former Chelsea players Dennis Wise and Tore Andre Flo."

Of course, not every boy or girl is Chelsea bonkers (hard to believe, we know), but that doesn't matter – they can still have a great time looking round a proper football club.

"Everyone is welcome - but we do point out various facts about Chelsea being better," says Wes, with a smile.

The birthday bashes are well received by parents and the partygoers alike. "The feedback afterwards is excellent," says Wesley. "The children really enjoy it. Most of the parties that are booked here are through word of mouth, people passing on the message that they had a great time."

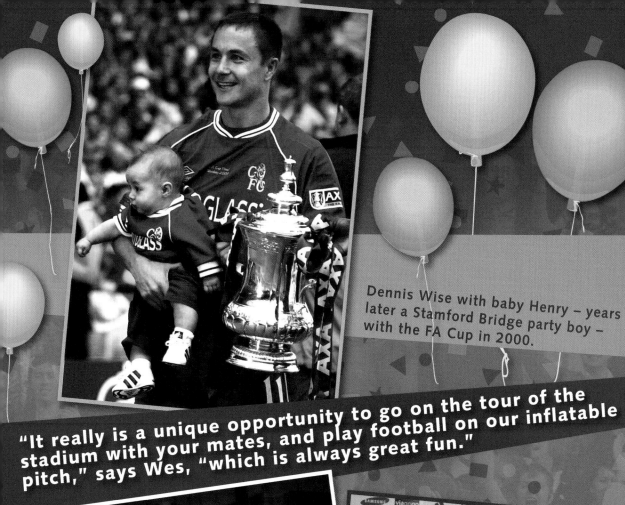

Dennis Wise with baby Henry – years later a Stamford Bridge party boy – with the FA Cup in 2000.

"It really is a unique opportunity to go on the tour of the stadium with your mates, and play football on our inflatable pitch," says Wes, "which is always great fun."

- The Chelsea FC Birthday Party Package is recommended for children aged 7-12.
- Each party includes:
  - » Chelsea FC-themed invitations.
  - » A fully guided tour of the legendary stadium.
  - » A supervised 5-a-side game of footy on an inflatable pitch.
  - » A Chelsea Gift.
  - » A birthday card for birthday boy/girl.
- Official certificates for all children taking part.
- Minimum 10 children per package; maximum 20.
- Minimum one adult for every five children.
- Parties go on sale one month in advance, feel free to enquire about available dates before that time.

Hot Tweets from Stamford The Lion!

From his favourite tree in the Cobham training ground, Stamford The Lion has a sneaky view of everything that is going on behind the scenes with the players. Luckily for us, he writes all about it on the internet!

The Chelsea mascot puts his stories, or 'tweets', up on the Twitter website for everyone to look at, and he is often ahead of the TV and newspapers with his scoops!

The Chelsea Twitter account is like an online diary, packed with short messages from Stamford saying what he has seen or been doing around Cobham. It's free, so go to the following address:

twitter.com/stamfordthelion

You can just read the tweets as you go, or open a free account (ask permission from your parent or guardian first) and be alerted when there is another piece of hot Chelsea news.

TWEET!

"I have just heard we are about to make an announcement" 10:00 AM, Jun 1st
"Carlo Ancelotti is the new Chelsea manager" 10:03 AM, Jun 1st

TWEET!

"Half-time, it's very hot here at Wembley. Especially being a lion" 3:59PM, May 30th
"We're FA Cup Champions 2009!" 4:58PM, May 30th

TWEET!

"John Terry has just won the 2009 Cobham Pool Tournament, beating Chelsea TV commentator Ben Andrews in the Final" 10:51 AM, May 29th

TWEET!

"Big Pete Cech has been handing round birthday cake in the canteen" 2:20 PM, May 20th

How would you like your tour?

ORIGINAL STADIUM TOUR

This un-missable, behind-the-scenes visit to the home of 'The Blues' is tailored to sport fans of all ages, from all over the world.

TOUR & LUNCH PACKAGE

Take your time at Stamford Bridge with a stadium tour combined with a delicious lunch at Frankie's Sports Bar and Grill

LEGENDS TOUR

Always popular, the Legend Tours give an amazing insight into the world of Chelsea FC from the eyes of a true Chelsea legend.

PLATINUM TOUR

Enjoy the personal touch with a private tour of Stamford Bridge. These tours allow up to 10 people per tour and include your own tour guide.

CHILDREN'S PARTIES

Stamford Bridge offers a unique setting for a truly memorable birthday and the best part is, you can leave it to us on the day!

With a wide range of tour options to suit everyone, there has never been a better time to take a tour of the famous Stamford Bridge; you just need to decide which one suits you best. All tours include entry to the Chelsea FC museum.

To book your tour
call **0871 984 1955** (during office hours)
email **tours@chelseafc.com**
or visit **www.chelseafc.com/tours**

CHELSEA FOOTBALL CLUB

Have your photo taken with the FA Cup!
Now available in the Chelsea Museum

Tours do not run on home matchdays or the day before Champions League games. All tours and photo opportunities are subject to availability and change.

CHELSEA HISTORY
FORTY YEARS AGO - OUR FIRST FA CUP!

2010 brings the 40th anniversary of one of the most famous chapters in the Chelsea story: our first ever victory in the FA Cup, way back in April 1970.

It is one of the most famous cup finals of all time, partly because it was the first for ages to require a replay after a draw at Wembley. But mostly it is remembered because it was played between two of the most famous clubs of the day, with two very different reputations, and a grudge against each other.

Chelsea were glamorous Londoners who spent nights out in fashionable clubs, and played exciting, inconsistent football. Leeds were a team from the north who ground out results and preferred to stay in playing bingo!

The first match of the final was played at Wembley Stadium on 11 April 1970. The pitch was terrible because horse hoofs from a recent show jumping event had cut up the surface. The football wasn't much better! It was a bad-tempered game with lots of fouls. Chelsea right-back David Webb was given the runaround by tricky Leeds winger Eddie Gray. The Whites led twice but goals from Peter Houseman and Ian Hutchinson made it 2-2 after extra time. A replay was needed.

Chelsea fans made the most of the day out at Wembley. It was the Blues' second FA Cup final in four years, but only our third ever, and manager Dave Sexton had built a brilliant team that is much loved by supporters to this day.

Chelsea 2 Leeds United 1
Scorers: Peter Osgood,
David Webb; Mick Jones (Leeds United)
Venue: Old Trafford
Attendance: 62,078
Date: 29 April 1970

The first half of the replay at Old Trafford was a bad one for Chelsea. Our heroic goalkeeper Peter Bonetti had been hurt in a challenge, and Mick Jones had scored for Leeds. Then with 12 minutes to go Peter Osgood headed in Charlie Cooke's brilliant cross to level the scores. Leeds heads dropped as the game went into extra time – again.

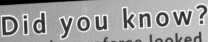

Did you know?

A modern referee looked at video of the Wembley match and said he would have sent off half the players on either side: it was such a dirty game!

Tormented in the Wembley game, Dave Webb became Chelsea's hero during extra time in the replay. When Ian Hutchinson's trademark long throw was knocked on, Webby rose at the far post to head in what would become the winning goal. He went bonkers!

Leeds had no reply to Webby's goal, and Chelsea won 2-1. Ron Harris became the first ever Chelsea skipper to lift the FA Cup. The team returned to London by train the following day and tens of thousands of supporters greeted them around Stamford Bridge. It is a game that will never be forgotten.

SIMPLY THE BEST!

Back in May 2009 the great and the good of Chelsea gathered in the Great Hall at Stamford Bridge for the annual Awards Evening. There was no argument about the winner of the top prize, and it was nice to see Ash's best season in blue recognised by his team-mates.

GOAL OF THE SEASON
MICHAEL ESSIEN VS BARCELONA

"It is always good to win something. We put effort in to win trophies and win personal trophies, so it is great. When I saw the ball coming that was the only option that came to my mind, I tried to take it and I had a bit of luck. It is difficult to score those kinds of goals and you need a bit of luck."

Michael Essien on his Champions League wonderstrike.

ADIDAS YOUNG PLAYER
MICHAEL MANCIENNE

This was chosen by two coaches who have worked closely with the first team and reserves, Paul Clement and Ray Wilkins. The winner, Michael Mancienne, had a great first half of the season on loan at Wolves, turned 21, and made his full Chelsea debut in the crucial replay at Watford – where his former boss at Chelsea, Brendan Rodgers, was in charge! Michael was a late sub in the Champions League too, against Juventus. He is a very versatile and cool-headed player, and was even called up to the full England squad in November 2008.

JT was presented with an award marking his ten years as a Chelsea Blue.

**PLAYER OF THE SEASON
FRANK LAMPARD**

"It feels great because of the amount of top quality players who have won this award. When I came here I never expected to win it three times at all, I just wanted to establish myself, but getting this award and the recognition from your own fans is a huge thing in football. I am absolutely delighted."

Frank Lampard on winning the evening's top prize, the Player of the Season award.

"I'm shocked but it's a great honour and I am very privileged to have got this award. There are a lot of players who deserved it, but I am happy to collect this award. It is always nice to get recognition from anyone but from your players it means a lot more."

SAMSUNG PLAYERS' PLAYER OF THE SEASON - ASHLEY COLE

CHELSEA'S
WORLD CUP STARS

In the last 60 years, Chelsea have sent more than 40 players from three different continents off to World Cup finals. Twelve have represented England, including our proud captain of club and country, John Terry. The nation with the next highest number of Chelsea representatives is France, with five. Let's look back at some of the Chelsea World Cup highlights over the years...

THE FIRST WORLD CUP BLUE...

Roy Bentley became the first Chelsea player to figure at a World Cup in 1950 when he played two full games for England in Brazil. That tournament is best remembered for a defeat by the United States that shocked the world of football. But Roy always served his country with distinction, scoring nine goals in 12 appearances.

HIGHEST WORLD CUP APPEARANCE-MAKER...

Marcel Desailly played more World Cup matches while with Chelsea than any other player: ten, in the 1998 and 2002 finals. The France central defender, known as 'The Rock', signed just before winning the World Cup final at France '98, and became a brilliant captain for Chelsea.

FIRST CHELSEA HOMEGROWN

At Mexico 1970 Peter Bonetti became the first former Blues youth team player to be chosen for a World Cup final squad while still at Stamford Bridge. Now John Terry follows in the great goalkeeper's footsteps.

HIGHEST GOALSCORER AT WORLD CUP FINALS...

Argentina's Hernán Crespo has scored the most goals at World Cup finals of any Blues player. His three goals all came at the 2006 tournament in Germany, at which his country reached the quarter-finals.

Here's a list of every Chelsea player who has been part of a World Cup squad, with their appearances and goals totals.

Celestine Babayaro - Nigeria
World Cup 1998 3 0
World Cup 2002 2 0

Michael Ballack - Germany
World Cup 2006 5 0

Dave Beasant - England
World Cup 1990 unused

Roy Bentley - England
World Cup 1950 2 0

Peter Bonetti - England
World Cup 1966 unused
World Cup 1970 1 0

Peter Brabrook - England
World Cup 1958 1 0

Wayne Bridge - England
World Cup 2006 unused

Ricardo Carvalho - Portugal
World Cup 2006 6 0

**Tony Cascarino
– Republic of Ireland**
World Cup 1994 unused

Petr Cech – Czech Republic
World Cup 2006 3 0

Joe Cole – England
World Cup 2006 5 1

Hernán Crespo – Argentina
World Cup 2006 4 3

Ed de Goey - Netherlands
World Cup 1998 unused

Marcel Desailly - France
World Cup 1998 7 0
World Cup 2002 3 0

Roberto Di Matteo - Italy
World Cup 1998 1+1 0

Kerry Dixon - England
World Cup 1986 0+1 0

Tony Dorigo - England
World Cup 1990 1 0

Didier Drogba – Ivory Coast
World Cup 2006 2 1

Gordon Durie - Scotland
World Cup 1990 1 0

Michael Essien - Ghana
World Cup 2006 3 0

Paulo Ferreira - Portugal
World Cup 2006 1+2 0

Albert Ferrer - Spain
World Cup 1998 1 0

Tore André Flo - Norway
World Cup 1998 4 1

William Gallas - France
World Cup 2006 7 0

Jesper Grønkjær - Denmark
World Cup 2002 3+1 0

Robert Huth - Germany
World Cup 2006 1 0

Erland Johnsen - Norway
World Cup 1994 1 0

Dmitri Kharine - Russia
World Cup 1994 2 0

Frank Lampard - England
World Cup 2006 5 0

Brian Laudrup - Denmark
World Cup 1998 5 2

Frank Lebœuf - France
World Cup 1998 2+1 0

Graeme Le Saux - England
World Cup 1998 4 0

Claude Makelele - France
World Cup 2006 7 0

Peter Osgood - England
World Cup 1970 0+2 0

Emmanuel Petit - France
World Cup 2002 2 0

Dan Petrescu- Romania
World Cup 1998 4 1

Arjen Robben - Netherlands
World Cup 2006 3 1

Andriy Shevchenko - Ukraine
World Cup 2006 5 2

Frank Sinclair - Jamaica
World Cup 1998 3 0

Mario Stanic - Croatia
World Cup 2002 0+2 0

John Terry - England
World Cup 2006 5 0

The Johnny Vaughan Q&A

Johnny Vaughan's links with the football team he loves – The Blues, of course – just got stronger. The 95.8 Capital FM breakfast show presenter is also a frontman for 'Help A London Child', Chelsea's new national charity partner. Here, he tells us about school food-fights, Frankie's penalty, and taking Megan Fox to the Bridge...

What is your earliest memory of being a Chelsea fan?

People forget that the word 'fan' is short for fanatic so this is a tricky one. I first started following Chelsea when I was about six, then supported them through the yo-yo years - but I wouldn't say I was a 'fan' until 1994. I'd been to every home and away game that season but couldn't get a ticket for Oxford United when we played them away in the FA Cup. Standing in the drizzle outside the gates of OUFC – having driven all the way up there – and hanging around for 90 minutes, following the game via the chanting inside and someone with a radio outside, was when it occurred to me that perhaps I'd turned the corner from supporter to fanatic.

What sports were you good at in your youth?

I used to love playing all sports in my youth until I snapped my anterior cruciate ligament and after two operations still couldn't trust my knee in a 50-50 challenge. My proudest sporting moment was probably after my school's regular centre-forward had been banned for four games following a food fight at a team tea. I took his place in the side and scored a hat-trick on my debut against our big rival school. My dad was there to witness it and I don't think I've ever seen him so proud.

> "...when it occurred to me that perhaps I'd turned the corner from supporter to fanatic."

Who would you most like to bring to Stamford Bridge?

Megan Fox. I met her the other day, and I think she'd really dig it - but that's not the main reason. I just think turning up to watch football with Megan giving it the 'no big deal' to the season ticket holders around me would be hilarious. If not her, Maradona would be a wild card guest.

Which Chelsea stars from any era would be your ideal breakfast show guests?

Jimmy Greaves, Tommy Docherty, Terry Venables, Vinnie Jones and Ruud Gullit. I wouldn't need many questions, I'd just start them off with a simple, "So what do you see as the problem facing the modern game?" and that's 24-hour radio.

Who was your first great Blues hero?
I loved Ray Wilkins when I was a lad but my all-time Blues hero would have to be Gianfranco Zola - a man who was simply all that a player should be. Footballer first, professional second, capable of producing both heart-stopping moments of individual skill and genuinely astounding team play. Aside from his dazzling footwork, out-of-nowhere goals, consistency, modesty, unselfishness, and the sheer entertainment he provided, I loved watching Zola because he was a man who clearly loved playing 'the game' of football.

What is your all-time favourite Chelsea moment?

Frank Lampard's extra-time penalty against Liverpool in the Champions League semi-final at The Bridge must rank as one of professional football's greatest moments of 'grace under pressure'. Frank's mum Pat had died just days before after a short illness. This was his first time back. The score was 2-2. A place in the Champions League final was at stake. It was the most important moment in the history of the club. Ballack was fouled. He could have taken the penalty but Frank took that ball, looked to the heavens and dedicated the penalty to his mum. When he hammered it home, not a critic or cynic in British football could deny his courage. That is a professional footballer. That is grace under pressure.

What tune should Chelsea run out to?

Harry J Allstars – 'Liquidator.' Why mess with a classic?

Have you ever secretly re-organised your work schedule so you could watch the Blues play in Europe?

In 1998 we hosted the 'Big Breakfast' TV show from Stansted Airport so I didn't miss the final of the European Cup Winners' Cup in Stockholm.

And what do you expect from season 2009/10 under Carlo Ancelotti?

Who knows? That's what keeps me going every week.

What are you most looking forward to from the Chelsea/Help A London Child link-up?

Many children live below the poverty line, need specialist treatment, or protection from abuse. Thousands just need a place they can feel safe. With London's biggest club behind us, we can hopefully tackle some of London's biggest issues.

Web link: www.capitalfm.com/helpalondonchild

GUESS WHO?

Can you identify the four Chelsea players hidden below?

A — anelka

B — Terry

C — mapelitoe

D — carvhalo

Do you think I am thick

Answers P.60

WORD SEARCH

There are 20 names of teams that have competed in the World Cup mixed up in the grid below. They go up, down, and diagonally. Can you spot them all? Which ~~country~~ has since changed its name?

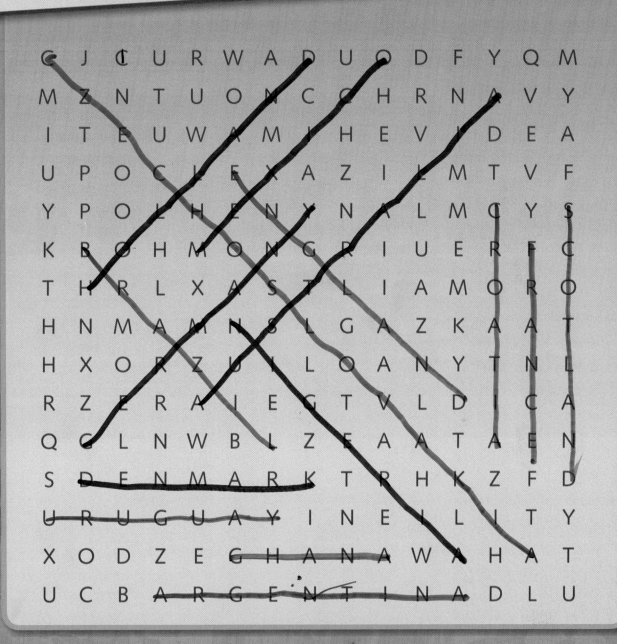

C J C U R W A D U O D F Y Q M
M Z N T U O N C C H R N A V Y
I T E U W A M I H E V I D E A
U P O C I E X A Z I L M T V F
Y P O L H E N Y N A L M C Y S
K B R H M O N G R I U E R F C
T H R L X A S T L I A M O R O
H N M A M N S L G A Z K A A T
H X O R Z U L O A N Y T N L
R Z E R A I E G T V L D I C A
Q C L N W B L Z E A A T A E N
S D E N M A R K T R H K Z F D
U R U G U A Y I N E L L I T Y
X O D Z E G H A N A W A H A T
U C B A R G E N T I N A D L U

ENGLAND   BRAZIL   SCOTLAND   ARGENTINA
BELGIUM   MEXICO   NIGERIA   HOLLAND
CROATIA   FRANCE   NORWAY   GERMANY
ITALY   URUGUAY   CZECHOSLOVAKIA   AUSTRALIA
ROMANIA   DENMARK   GHANA   CHILE

Answers P.61

41

Help a London Child!

Back in May Chelsea FC announced a new national charity partner. 'Help a London Child' is an organisation set up by London radio station 95.8 Capital FM. Together, Chelsea and Help a London Child aim to raise a lot of money to bring some joy to the lives of children who have experienced all sorts of problems.

DID YOU KNOW?
The founder and Life Patron of 95.8 Capital FM's Help a London Child is Lord Attenborough CBE – who is also Chelsea's Life President!

95.8 CAPITAL FM's HELP A LONDON CHILD gives money to projects helping young people who need support throughout London. All of the players will be involved in publicising the fundraising, and there will be plenty of opportunities for you to join in and help out.

Funnily enough, 95.8 Capital FM Breakfast Show presenter Johnny Vaughan is a lifelong Blue too. He was very excited at the announcement. "As a supporter of both Chelsea and Help a London Child, to me this is an ideal partnership," said Johnny, "the two best teams in London are joining forces to help London's children."

Chelsea's captain and hero JT backed him up. "We are in a fortunate position to be able to help good causes," said John. "The whole team is looking forward to supporting Help a London Child and the fantastic work it does with kids."

HELP A LONDON CHILD

95.8 Capital FM's Help a London Child (registered charity number 1091657) was launched in 1975 by Lord Attenborough, CBE. Over the last thirty-four years, the charity has raised in excess of £20m and awarded more than 10,000 grants to small groups and charities, working with London's less well-off and most vulnerable young people. For more information on 95.8 Capital FM's Help a London Child visit: www.capitalfm.com/helpalondonchild

DID YOU KNOW?
Within London you are never more than a mile from a project supported by 95.8 Capital FM's Help a London Child.

DID YOU KNOW?
A charity is an organisation set up to help a particular group of people or animals in need. Charities rely on fundraising and volunteers – including many children - to carry out their vital work.

VERY BIG DEAL
IN AMERICA

Chelsea toured the USA for the third time this summer, and boy was it worth it! Four wins in four cities, amazing stadiums, huge sell-out crowds everywhere, and great Chelsea performances.

THAT'S BALL MINE! At an open training session attended by around 4,000 local supporters, the players kicked balls into the stands. The lucky ones celebrated their catch!

BACK IN THE OLD ROUTINE Wherever Petr Cech and his teammates travelled around the United States, there was always a shirt to be autographed...

8 + 8 = LEGENDS
Chelsea no.8 Frank Lampard met the man who wears that number for American Football team Seattle Seahawks, Matt Hasselbeck, and they exchanged tips on how to pass the two different-shaped balls.

And Didier soon got into his goalscoring stride against Inter.

TALKING FRANKLY Local station ESPN asked former Chelsea legend Frank Leboeuf (left) to interview new Blues manager Carlo Ancelotti in Seattle.

A SPECIAL MOMENT
Before the match with Inter there was time to greet an old friend: José Mourinho, who now manages the Italian club Inter Milan.

SUPER STARS
Top American comedy star Will Ferrell, a big Chelsea fan, was allowed to perform the coin toss before kick-off against Inter.

Hollywood star Charlize Theron was proud of her new Chelsea shirt.

Actor Ashton Kutcher watched the game from the end of the Chelsea bench, lucky boy!

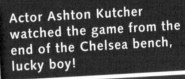

BIG RESPONSE
Everywhere the boys went there were Chelsea In America supporters cheering them on.

YURI ONE OF US
NOW Like fellow new boy Danny Sturridge, Yuri Zhirkov scored on his Chelsea debut against AC Milan and was mobbed by teammates.

ENJOYING THE SUN
The USA was the ideal place to warm-up before the season started, with the weather and facilities just perfect.

SPOT THE BALL

Study the picture below closely, then use your skill to spot where you think the ball might be?

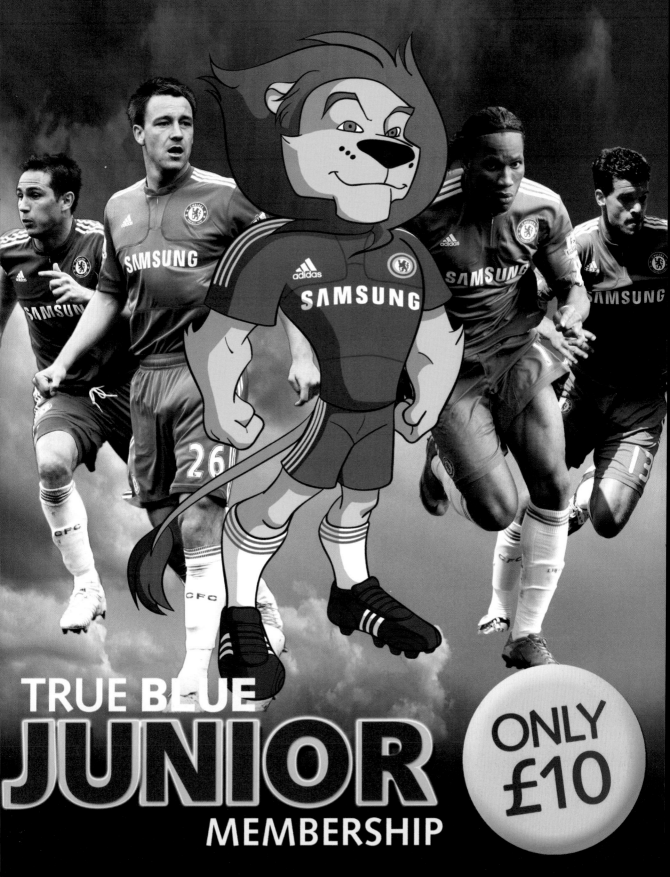

CROSSWORD

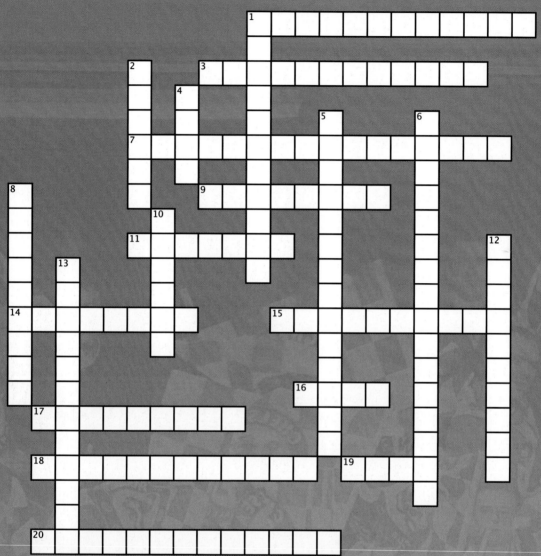

Across

1. Oversized keeper from 1905
3. Has won Player of the Year a record three times
7. Young Player of the Year 2009
9. Italian club previously managed by Carlo Ancelotti
11. Chelsea shirt sponsor
14. 1980s winger who writes a column on the official website
15. Spanish team we beat in the 1971 Uefa Cup-Winners' Cup final
16. Number of times we have won the FA Cup
17. All-time top-scoring defender
18. National rail station closest to Stamford Bridge
19. _ _ _ _ Canoville, first black first team player
20. 2009 Golden Boot winner

Down

1. Monument to striker George Hilsdon on top of the east stand
2. Dermot _ _ _ _ _ _, Chelsea Academy team manager
4. Bruce _ _ _ _, Chelsea chairman
5. The north stand is named after him
6. Club's new charity partner
8. Beaten opponents in Champions League quarter-final 2009
10. City that will host the 2010 Champions League final
12. Chelsea TV show for younger fans
13. Goalie nicknamed 'The Cat'

STAMFORD'S GUIDE TO ...

Next summer the world's greatest football tournament, the World Cup, comes to my homeland, and I can't wait! It is the first time the finals have been held in Africa and it looks like all the top teams will be there too. As an African lion I may be biased, but I reckon it'll be the best ever, and here's why...

SA Organising committee president Dr Danny Jordaans with Clarence Seedorf

SOUTH AFRICA FACT FILE

» The population of SA is around 48m people.
» Its largest city is Johannesburg.
» The most famous South African is Nelson Mandela.
» SA is one of the richest countries in Africa.
» It is famous for its wildlife (including lions!) and safari holidays.
» South Africans love music and dancing.

AMAZING STARS: Every four years the World Cup brings together the best players on the planet. This one is likely to feature greats such as Kaka, Lionel Messi, Franck Ribéry, as well as Chelsea legends like Didier Drogba, Michael Essien, John Terry and Frank Lampard.

...THE FIFA 2010 WORLD CUP IN SOUTH AFRICA

A WHOLE MONTH OF FOOTY: The opening match will feature South Africa, the host nation, on 11 June 2010, and the final will take place at the 94,000-seater Soccer City stadium in Johannesburg. There are 32 teams, ten stadiums, and more matches than I can count on four paws. It's going to be amazing.

BRAND NEW STADIUMS: Wow! Three brand new, state-of-the-art arenas are being built to host the World Cup matches in South Africa, including this one in Durban with 100m tall arches. It will be called the Moses Madibha stadium.

CRAZY SUPPORTERS: South African people love football and will fill the stadiums. They make a lot of noise at matches and dress in weird ways to show support for local teams such as Kaizer Chiefs. Bet you didn't know the English band Kaiser Chiefs are named after a South African football club!

A REALLY WILD MASCOT - ZAKUMI

I have to admit Zakumi is a cool dude for a mascot, even though he's a leopard and not a lion – only joking! His name comes from Z.A., which is the international code for South Africa, and 'kumi', which means ten. So Zakumi actually means 'South Africa ten'.

FA COMMUNITY SHIELD 2009

Chelsea have now claimed the Shield four times: the last time we won it, in 2005, we went on to win the Premier League.

CHELSEA 2
MANCHESTER UNITED 2
(Chelsea win 4-1 on penalties)
Venue: Wembley Stadium
Scorers: Carvalho, Lampard;
Nani, Rooney
Date: 9 August 2009
Attendance: 85,896

Riccy's diving header brought Chelsea's well-deserved equaliser. His only goal last season was against United's big rivals, Man City.

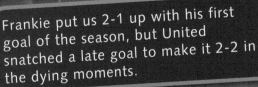

Frankie put us 2-1 up with his first goal of the season, but United snatched a late goal to make it 2-2 in the dying moments.

A trophy in his first proper match in charge! Carlo Ancelotti's start to his Chelsea managerial career was a special one. And he outwitted Fergie!

We won the Shield! JT and the chaps celebrate taking two trophies in three months, following the FA Cup back in May.

THE SHOOTOUT

After the game was drawn on 90 minutes, Chelsea won the penalty shootout 4-1. Amazingly, it was way back in 1998 that we were last victorious in one, against Ipswich Town in the League Cup. And it was a tiny bit of revenge for the Champions League final shootout loss, also against United.

I saved two Utd pens!
Petr reminds everyone he's the real shootout hero.

CHELSEA: Lampard ●   Ballack ●   Drogba ●   Kalou ●
UNITED: Giggs ●   Carrick ●   Evra ●

I scored the winning spot-kick! Salomon Kalou scoring the winning penalty in the shootout.

09 WINNERS

2008/09 STAT ATTACK!

Another great season
– we do the maths.

110 Goals scored

29 Clean sheets kept

Best away record in the Premier League: 44 points from 19 games, including 14 wins.

7 New club record for consecutive away clean sheets

19 League goals scored by Golden Boot winner Nicolas Anelka

100 Goals scored by Frank Lampard in five seasons

86 Home league games undefeated

61 Games without conceding a penalty

Season summary: Played 59, won 37, drawn 16, lost 6.

2008/09 FINAL STANDINGS

Premier League – third.
Champions League – semi-finalist (fifth time in six seasons).
League Cup – fourth round.
FA Cup – winners.

5 — FA Cup winner's medals for Ashley Cole.

Liverpool 1 Chelsea 3
Liverpool's worst ever European defeat at Anfield.

7,000 — Goals scored since 1905

400 — Frank Lampard and John Terry each passed the 400 mark for appearances in a Chelsea shirt

74 — Games undefeated in all competitions in Season 2008/09

87 — Percentage of points won in Guus Hiddink's first five matches

11 — New top-flight record of consecutive away wins

200 — Petr Cech and Didier Drogba each passed 200 appearances for Chelsea

Arsenal 1 Chelsea 4
Equalled our best away league win at Arsenal with 1959/60 and 1960/61.

Think You've Got the Skills?
Here's How To Impress Frank Arnesen!

If you are playing football regularly, or planning to, the chances are there will be a 'trial' or practice session at some stage where squad members will be selected. Whether it's for a local club/school team or a famous academy such as Chelsea's the chances are that the coaches will be looking for more or less the same things.

Who better than Chelsea's Sporting Director, Frank Arnesen, whose job it is to uncover talent from all age groups and bring it to Stamford Bridge, to provide some ideas that might just give you the edge when you try out.

At the younger end of the spectrum, Frank and his staff are very clear about what they look for in a player, besides obvious talent. "We talk about five main areas," says the Dane. "Technical, Tactical, Physical, Mental and Lifestyle – they're like the Olympic rings of football.

"Of course you take the technical side for granted by the time we see the children – although you should never stop working on it. But some of the other areas are clear when you think about them. Physically, for example, you cannot be too small if you would like to be a goalkeeper, or too slow in some positions. If you are small, you generally need to be quick, and if you are big and strong but lacking a little pace, you have to be clever."
Sometimes it is about adapting to what your body allows. "Take Maradona or Messi," says Frank. "They could not be centre-halves, but they are quick and clever and perfect for playing from the wing.

"Lifestyle too: everyone knows that you should avoid drugs and alcohol, which are a no-no for boys or girls who want to reach their potential. It is also about eating and drinking well. I was very bad when I was young. I liked fruit, which is good, but I didn't eat well and didn't like vegetables, not much fish. I learned about the importance of nutrition later, and that you need sleep."

Being focused and passionate about football, is what Frank values above all the other assets, because a positive attitude helps everything else.

"I think the most important one is desire, which is part of mentality," he says. "You must not be too arrogant, and be critical of yourself always, but do not lose self-confidence. Be flexible – everyone defends on the pitch nowadays. Never forget why you want to play at a top level – you have something others lack, whether it is skill or your attitude.

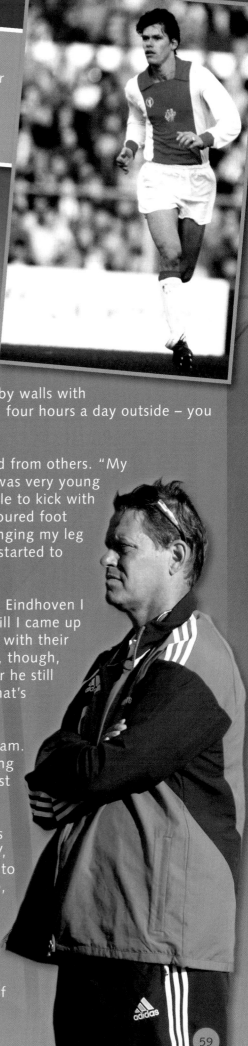

"You should always be listening and learning. Imagination, creativity – these are extremely valuable on a football pitch, and they come from desire."

Having the correct attitude from an early age is very important, and in the days when the streets are choked with cars, Frank recommends joining a local team rather than playing in the streets as he did when he was growing up in Denmark.

"We used to play in the street, kicking the ball up against a wall, working on our skills and competitiveness. There was a gravel area surrounded by walls with benches you could use as goals. We would play three, four hours a day outside – you cannot do that now."

Lessons on the technical and tactical side were learned from others. "My father played football too, and he said to me when I was very young that the most important thing was that I should be able to kick with both feet. He made me practice swinging my less-favoured foot so that it felt right. I remember running to school swinging my leg every few yards, without a ball, just so that my body started to feel balanced when I did it.

"When I was first asked to train the under-12s at PSV Eindhoven I started by working on their "other" foot. We did a drill I came up with and the following day two brothers were kicking with their left foot brilliantly. I thought I was a genius! One boy, though, he just didn't get it. I tried everything, but a year later he still looked strange when he kicked with his other foot. That's when I realised I wasn't a genius after all!"

Frank's father also taught him that a goal is for the team. "He always said that an assist is as important as scoring myself, which I enjoyed doing, as well as dribbling past as many players as I could."

One thing that is better for youngsters today is access to seeing their football heroes playing, whether on TV, DVD or the internet. Frank sees it as a big advantage to be able to see old footage of the masters of the game, "When I was young we would watch a match and spend two hours outside re-enacting the game," he smiles. He says it is a good idea to identify a player who you think plays in a similar way to you, and study them whenever you can. But don't copy endless stepovers, learn what they do, adapt it, and, if possible, make it even better.

 # QUIZ ANSWERS

BLUE SAID THAT?
from page 16

1. Temporary first team manager Guus Hiddink.
2. Assistant manager Ray Wilkins.
3. Frank Lampard.
4. Ashley Cole – who won three with Arsenal.
5. Michael Essien.

GUESS WHO?
from page 40

A — Nicolas Anelka

B — John Terry

C — Carlo Ancelotti

D — Ricardo Caravalho

WORD SEARCH

from page 41

```
C J C U R W A D U O D F Y Q M
M Z N T U O N C C H R N A V Y
I T E U W A M I H E V I D E A
U P O C L E X A Z I L M T V F
Y P O L H E N Y N A L M C Y S
K B O H M O N G R I U E C O
T H R L X A S T L I A M F R
H N M A M N S L G A Z K A A
H X O R Z U I L O A N Y T L N
R Z E R A I E G T V L D C A
Q G L N W B L Z E A A T E F D
S D E N M A R K T R H K Z I T
U R U G U A Y I N E I L I T Y
X O D Z E G H A N A W A H A T
U C B A R G E N T I N A D L U
```

Which country has since changed its name?
A: Czechoslovakia is now the Czech Republic

CROSSWORD

from page 50

```
                    W I L L I E F O U L K E
                    E
              F R A N K L A M P A R D
        D     E
        R  B  T
        U  U  H
        M  M  M I C H A E L M A N C I E N N E
        M  Y  R
           J U V E N T U S
L          M    A  M          P
I          A    N  T          A
V  S A M S U N G   E  H       L
E          R       W       O
R  P A T N E V I N D    H  R E A L M A D R I D
P  E                 A  R              R  B
O  R                 R  D    F I V E   I  R
O  B                 D       I         C  I
L  J O H N T E R R Y  I       G         H  D
   N                 N       W E S T B R O M P T O N  P A U L  G
   E                                               L  E
   T  W E S T B R O M P T O N                      D  K
   T                                                  I
   N I C O L A S A N E L K A                          D
                                                      S
```

from page 47

SPOT THE BALL

FA CUP GLORY

Chelsea won the FA Cup for the fifth time, Didier scored in his fifth cup final on the spin, and Lamps notched his 20th goal of the season. A brilliant day in the sunshine.

Chelsea 2

"They are worthy winners. Playing Chelsea was just a hurdle too much for us today. They were the better team"
– Everton boss, David Moyes